AF316825

The Little Book of the Sixteen Cs for a Happy Marriage

Also by Michael J. Lyons

Set Yourself Free:

Daydream It... Believe It... Achieve It!

The Little Book of

the Sixteen Cs

for a Happy Marriage

Simple Daily Habits That Help Love Last

by Michael J. Lyons

Foreword by John Quiñones

The Little Book of the Sixteen Cs for a Happy Marriage
Simple Daily Habits That Help Love Last

Published by Blue Bell Press
Philadelphia, Pennsylvania

ISBN: [HARDCOVER ISBN — 979-8-9955839-0-5]
ISBN: [PAPERBACK ISBN — 979-8-9955839-1-2]
ISBN: [EBOOK ISBN — 979-8-9955839-2-9]

Library of Congress Control Number: [2026908861]

Foreword by John Quiñones
Cover design by Jane Korunoski
Interior design and typesetting by Jane Korunoski

First Edition
Printed in the United States of America

10 9 8 7 6 5 4 3 2 1
www.The16Cs.com
info@the16cs.com

For Lorie

I dedicate this book to you, my beautiful and steadfast wife, Lorie.

Our courtship began on May 22, 1973. By October 22 of that same year, you had said "yes." On April 20, 1974, you became my wife — and on that day, without fully knowing it, we began an adventurous journey we could never have imagined.

What followed has not been a fairy tale. It is something better: life — real, full, and hard-won. We have weathered storms that tested us and savored seasons that surprised us. We have grieved, laughed, disagreed, and forgiven, choosing each other again and again on ordinary days more times than either of us can count.

We raised three children and watched them grow into people we are proud of. We have been blessed beyond measure with grandchildren who carry pieces of both of us forward into a future we will not fully see — and that is a gift we never take lightly.

Through every chapter, you have been my constant: my anchor when the water got rough and my rock when everything else shifted. You have loved me not as the man I imagined myself to be, but as the man I actually am — and somehow, in the shelter of that love, I became more of who I was always meant to be.

This book is about what it takes to build a lasting marriage. But the truth is, I did not write it as an expert; I wrote it as a student. And you have been my greatest teacher.

Every page of this book carries something of you in it. Every C begins with what I have watched you live.

This is for you, my darling Lorie. It has always been for you.

With all my love, now and always,

Your Michael

Table of Contents

Foreword

by John Quiñones

Over the years, through my work as a journalist and storyteller, I've had the privilege of witnessing human behavior in its most revealing moments — how people act when no one is watching, how they respond when faced with a choice between convenience and character.

What I've learned is this: who we are is most clearly seen in the small, everyday decisions we make. That truth doesn't just apply to strangers in public settings. It applies most powerfully in our closest relationships, especially in marriage.

Since 2014, I've had the pleasure of knowing Michael J. Lyons not only as a professional but as a friend. And in that time, I've come to respect something in him that cannot be manufactured or exaggerated — authenticity.

Michael doesn't speak about marriage as a theory or an academic exercise. He speaks about it as a man who has lived it, day in and day out, for more than fifty years. And that matters.

Because lasting relationships are not built on ideas alone. They are built on choices. Repeated choices. Quiet decisions made over time that shape the foundation of a life shared with another person.

What Michael has done in this book is both simple and meaningful. He has taken decades of lived experience and distilled it into sixteen guiding principles, each beginning with the letter "C," which reflect the habits, attitudes, and behaviors that help love endure.

These are not complicated concepts. They are accessible. Practical. Real.

The power of these ideas lies in their consistency – in the understanding that strong marriages are not built in a single moment, but over time, through small acts of patience, kindness, honesty, and commitment.

What I appreciate most about this book is that it does not attempt to present perfection. Instead, it offers something far more valuable – perspective.

A reminder that marriage is not about avoiding challenges, but about how we choose to meet them.

Whether you are just beginning your journey together or have been walking it for many years, this book offers something worth revisiting again and again. Because in the end, the strength of any relationship comes down to one simple truth:

What we do consistently matters more than what we do occasionally.

And as Michael reminds us so well — a happy marriage is not something we stumble upon. It is something we build.

— *John Quiñones*

Host, *What Would You Do?*

ABC News Correspondent

Introduction

Why the Cs Matter — and Why I Know

My wife and I have been married for fifty-two years.

That number means more to me than longevity alone. It means we have built a life through seasons of joy, stress, change, grief, success, setbacks, laughter, and countless ordinary days that never make the photo album but make a marriage what it is. We have raised children, faced financial pressures, buried loved ones, celebrated milestones, disagreed, forgiven, adapted, and kept choosing each other.

I did not write this book as a therapist, researcher, or academic observer. I wrote it as a husband who has spent a lifetime learning what helps love grow, and observing what slowly causes it to weaken.

Over the years, I began to notice that the strongest marriages are rarely built on grand romantic gestures alone. They are built on repeated habits. Small choices. Daily practices. Quiet disciplines.

Many of those habits can be described with one memorable letter: C.

For this book, I have organized these practices around sixteen C words. Not because marriage can be reduced to a formula — it cannot — but because love does leave clues. And when you notice the qualities that appear again and again in healthy, lasting relationships, you begin to see a pattern.

These are the Sixteen Cs:

- Compatibility
- Commitment
- Communication
- Consideration
- Compassion
- Compromise
- Concern
- Conciliation
- Courtesy
- Cooperation
- Caring
- Companionship
- Candor
- Courage
- Celebration
- Consistency

Think of these sixteen Cs as the architecture of a lasting home. Compatibility is the foundation. Commitment is the frame. The remaining fourteen are the walls, the windows, the roof — each one necessary, each one holding up the others. Remove one, and the structure weakens. Neglect several, and you have something that may still be standing but can no longer shelter anyone from the storm.

Whether you are newly in love or celebrating your fortieth anniversary, whether your relationship is thriving or struggling, the invitation of this book is the same: read, reflect, and ask yourself honestly which of these Cs you are practicing well and which ones deserve more of your attention. The answers may surprise you. They may also save you.

You do not need to master all sixteen overnight. You only need to begin.

This book is designed to be read quickly, returned to often, and shared easily. Each chapter offers one essential quality, a simple insight, a few practical reminders, and a short takeaway you can carry into real life.

Because real love is not built in one dramatic moment.

Real love is built on the small and necessary things, practiced over time.

1.

Compatibility

The right fit matters

My wife Lorie and I are not the same person. We never have been. She is measured where I am impulsive, patient where I am quick. There are things she loves that leave me cold, and things I love that she endures with gracious indifference. After fifty-two years, none of that has changed.

What has not changed, either, is this: we want the same life. We believe in the same things. We see faith, family, loyalty, and the future in ways that fit together rather than pull apart. That is compatibility – and it is why we are still here.

Chemistry may start a relationship, but compatibility helps sustain one.

Compatibility is not about liking all the same foods, shows, or hobbies. It is about whether two people can truly build a life together.

Do you share core values? Do you see money, family, faith, commitment, honesty, and the future in ways that can live side by side? Can your differences enrich the relationship instead of tearing it apart?

I remember a simple Saturday morning early in our marriage when nothing important was at stake, and yet we were completely out of sync. I had a plan for the day—things to get done, errands to run, a sense of moving forward. Lorie was moving at a different pace, grounded in the moment, focused on the children and whatever the morning was bringing.

There was no argument. No disagreement. Just a quiet tension that neither of us named. I felt it as frustration. She likely felt it as pressure. We were living in the same house but experiencing the moment in entirely different ways.

Looking back, that moment taught me something I didn't understand at the time: compatibility is not about moving at the same speed. It's about moving in the same direction.

Many couples confuse attraction with alignment. Attraction is exciting, but alignment is stabilizing.

Attraction may pull two people together. Compatibility helps them stay together.

A healthy marriage does not require two identical personalities. In fact, some differences create balance. One person may be more outgoing, the other more reflective. One may be the planner, the other the spontaneous spirit. Those differences can complement each other beautifully when deeper values are shared.

But when a couple is divided on non-negotiables, trouble begins. If one person wants children and the other does not, if one believes fidelity is sacred and the other treats it lightly, if one values stability and the other thrives on chaos, love alone may not be enough to bridge the gap.

The beginning of a relationship is the time to have these conversations, however uncomfortable they may feel. Ask not just what your partner enjoys but what they believe. Ask not just where they want to vacation, but where they want to be in twenty years. Ask about money, faith, family loyalty, and the non-negotiables.

And then, equally important, listen to the answers. Not to what you hope the answers will be. Not to what you imagine you can eventually change. Listen to what is actually being said.

I have watched couples with electric chemistry and genuine love fail because they wanted fundamentally different lives and believed they could paper over the gap. I have watched couples who seemed mismatched from the outside build something extraordinary because their deeper values were perfectly aligned.

The lesson learned over a long time: love is not always enough. The right fit matters enormously.

Marriage works best when two people want the same kind of life and respect the way each other is built.

QUICK REMINDERS

- Shared values matter more than shared hobbies.
- Personality differences can work when respect is strong.
- Unspoken incompatibilities do not disappear after the wedding

ASK YOURSELVES

What matters most to each of us, and are we building in the same direction?

LITTLE TRUTH TO KEEP

A lasting marriage needs more than just sparks. It requires a good fit.

2.

Commitment

Love chooses to stay

Commitment is the decision — made not once but repeatedly, often quietly, sometimes with great difficulty — to stay. To invest. To choose this person and this relationship above the competing claims of easier paths, shinier options, temporary frustrations, and the seductive fantasy that somewhere out there is a more perfect partner waiting to be discovered.

In a society that values freedom and options above everything else, commitment has become unfashionable. We like to keep our choices open, to avoid being locked in, to leave when things stop being easy. And yet the couples who have the deepest satisfaction and the greatest joy are not the ones who stayed because they had to. They are the ones who stayed because they chose to. There is a world of difference between those two things.

There was a period in our marriage when life felt especially full — work demands, family responsibilities, and the constant movement that comes with raising children. Nothing was wrong, but everything required energy. It would have been easy in that season to drift into parallel lives, each of us focused on simply getting through the day.

I remember one evening in particular when we were both tired, the kind of tiredness that makes even small conversations feel like effort. It would have been easy to let the night pass quietly, each of us retreating into our own space. Instead, Lorie sat down and simply said, "Let's not lose each other in all of this."

It wasn't dramatic. It wasn't emotional. But it was a choice. A quiet decision to stay connected when it would have been easier not to. Looking back, I realize that commitment often looks exactly like that — not a grand declaration, but a small moment where one person chooses the relationship again.

True commitment is not a cage. It is a container — a structure within which trust can deepen, vulnerability can be risked, and love can mature into something far richer than the intoxicating early weeks of romantic infatuation. It is only within committed relationships that we discover who we truly are, because it is only there that we cannot hide. The person who sees us at our worst, who knows our fears and failures, who has watched us through illness and disappointment and the ordinary exhaustion of a Wednesday afternoon — that person's continued love means something that no amount of admiration from strangers can match.

Commitment also means choosing your partner not as the idealized version you fell in love with, but as the real, flawed, evolving person they are and are becoming. People change. They grow in unexpected directions. They develop new passions and let go of old ones. Commitment is not the promise to love a frozen snapshot of who your partner was on your wedding day. It is the promise to keep showing up as they become who they are meant to be.

Most importantly, commitment does not mean tolerating the intolerable. It does not mean staying in abuse or betrayal without consequence. In a healthy marriage, commitment means that difficulty does not automatically lead to departure.

The strongest couples are not the ones who never struggle. They are the ones who decide the struggle will be faced together.

QUICK REMINDERS

- Commitment is a repeated choice, not a one-time speech.
- Security grows when both partners know the marriage is worth fighting for.
- What you feed grows — including your relationship.

ASK YOURSELVES

How do we show each other that this marriage is a priority, not a convenience?

LITTLE TRUTH TO KEEP

Commitment says: I am with you, especially when life is hard.

3.

Communication

Speak honestly. Listen fully.

Communication is the circulatory system of a relationship. Just as blood carries oxygen to every organ in the body, honest and frequent communication carries understanding, connection, and repair to every corner of a partnership. When communication flows freely, problems are caught early, resentments dissolve before they calcify, and intimacy deepens over time. When it stops flowing, everything begins to die — slowly, and then, in the end, suddenly.

Effective communication in relationships is not simply talking. It is talking and listening in equal measure, with the willingness to be genuinely changed by what you hear. Most people, when their partner is speaking, are not truly listening — they are planning their response, waiting for a pause to make their point, or privately rehearsing how they were right. This kind of pseudo-listening is worse than silence because it creates the illusion of connection while actually deepening the distance.

For me, this has always been a weakness. Over the years, I've had conversations that should have been simple but weren't. Lorie would be trying to tell me something that mattered to her — not urgent, not dramatic, but important. I heard the words, but I wasn't really paying attention. I was already forming my response, thinking ahead to what I wanted to say, or worse, just tuning out.

And she has had to repeatedly call me out on it: "You're not hearing me," she will say. Not in frustration, not sharply — just clearly. And she's right. I am present in those conversations, but not engaged in them.

These moments resonate with me and point out a flaw that many of us share. They reveal something crucial in a relationship: communication isn't about participating. It's about understanding. And those are not the same thing.

Communication does more than resolve problems — it shapes the entire emotional climate of a marriage. Over time, the way two people speak to each other becomes the atmosphere they live in. Encouraging words create safety. Dismissive or critical ones create distance. And small patterns, repeated daily, quietly determine whether a relationship feels like a place of support or a place of tension. It is not just what we say in big moments that matters, but what we say — and how we say it — in the ordinary ones.

Another truth that often goes unnoticed is that communication is not always about solving anything. Many conflicts in marriage are not problems to be fixed, but experiences to be understood. One person speaks not because they need an answer, but because they need to feel heard. And when that need is missed — when listening turns into correcting, advising, or defending — frustration grows on both sides. Sometimes the most powerful response in a marriage is not a solution, but a simple acknowledgment: "I understand." That moment, small as it seems, can defuse tension, build trust, and strengthen connection in a way that no perfect answer ever could.

True listening requires the temporary suspension of your own perspective. It requires the curiosity to ask: What is this person actually experiencing? What are they trying to tell me? Not: How do I defend myself? Not: When is it my turn? When communication is healthy, small misunderstandings stay small. Resentments are addressed before they harden. Intimacy deepens because both people feel known.

Authentic communication requires honesty. “I’m fine” is one of the most dangerous sentences in marriage when it is not true. Honest communication sounds more like this: “I feel hurt.” “I need more from us.” “I am worried.” “Can we talk?”

When communication weakens, distance grows quietly. Couples stop saying what they feel, what they fear, what they need, and what they hope. They settle for routine exchanges and careful half-truths. Outwardly, the marriage may look intact. Inwardly, the connection begins to thin.

Tone matters. Timing matters. Repair matters. Not every conversation should happen in the heat of frustration. Sometimes wisdom says, “This matters. Let’s come back to it when we can really talk.”

A strong marriage is not built by avoiding hard conversations. It is built by learning how to have them well.

QUICK REMINDERS

- Listening is not waiting for your turn to speak.
- Silence can be more damaging than conflict.
- Repair after an argument is one of marriage's most important skills.

ASK YOURSELVES

What truth have we been avoiding that would bring us closer if we finally said it kindly?

LITTLE TRUTH TO KEEP

Real intimacy begins when truth can be spoken safely.

4.

Consideration

Love pays attention

Consideration is the daily practice of taking your spouse into account. It is the art of paying attention – not just to what your partner says but to what they need, what they feel, what costs them energy and what restores it. It is the decision, made dozens of times a day, to factor your partner's experience into your choices rather than treating them as background scenery in the story of your own life.

This sounds obvious. In practice, it is one of the most commonly neglected qualities in long-term relationships, because it requires a kind of ongoing attention that does not come naturally to most of us. We are, by default, the center of our own experience. Our own needs feel urgent and real. Our partner's needs, especially when we're tired, stressed, or preoccupied, can fade into abstraction.

A while back, I remember a small moment that I almost missed entirely. We were getting ready to go out, nothing special, just a simple evening. I was focused on the timing, the logistics, making sure we left when I thought we should. Lorie was moving a little more slowly, quieter than usual, but I didn't register it at first.

At one point she paused and said, almost offhandedly, "I've had a long day." It wasn't a complaint. It wasn't a request. Just a statement. And for a second, I nearly let it pass — another piece of information in a busy moment.

But something made me stop. I asked a simple question, and then another. And as she answered, I realized how close I had come to missing it entirely — the opportunity to shift the evening, to slow things down, to make it easier instead of pushing forward with my plan.

That's what consideration often is: not a big decision, but a moment of awareness. A pause. A choice to notice.

Consideration does more than make a relationship pleasant — it makes it secure. Over time, the small signals of attentiveness between two people answer an unspoken but constant question: *Do I matter here?* When those signals are present — when a partner notices, adjusts, and responds — the answer becomes clear. And that clarity creates emotional safety. People relax in relationships where they feel seen. They open up more. They give more. They trust more. Without that steady sense of being considered, even a loving relationship can begin to feel uncertain, as if something important is missing but hard to name.

There is also a subtle but powerful truth about consideration: it is rarely requested. Most of the time, your partner will not say, "Please think of me here." They will adapt, adjust, or stay silent. That is why consideration requires initiative. It asks you to notice without being prompted, to respond without being reminded. And over time, that kind of awareness becomes one of the clearest expressions of love. Not because it is dramatic, but because it is chosen — again and again — in moments where it would have been easier not to think beyond yourself.

Consideration means bringing your partner back into focus. It means asking, before you make plans, whether those plans work for them as well. It means noticing when they seem off and asking about it rather than waiting for them to raise it. It means remembering that the person you love has an inner life that is just as rich, just as complex, and just as deserving of your attention as your own.

Being considerate shows up in the smallest details. Turning down the television when they're on a work call. Refilling their coffee without being asked. Choosing the restaurant they'll enjoy rather than the one you prefer. Offering to drive when they're tired. Going to the museum together instead of playing golf for the third Saturday in a row. None of these are heroic acts. Taken together, over years, they are the steady accumulation of one message: I see you. You matter to me. I am paying attention.

Selfishness is natural. Consideration is intentional.

In many marriages, love weakens not because of dramatic harm, but because one or both partners begin moving through life as if the other person is expected to adapt automatically. Consideration interrupts that drift.

Thoughtful love often speaks in small actions before it ever speaks in words.

QUICK REMINDERS

- Consideration lives in small moments.
- Thoughtlessness can wound even where love exists.
- To be considered is to feel valued.

ASK YOURSELVES

What small adjustment could I make this week that would lighten my spouse's load?

LITTLE TRUTH TO KEEP

Love feels warm when it feels thought of.

5.

Compassion

Be tender with each other

Compassion is the ability to see your spouse's pain and respond with warmth and kindness rather than judgment, with closeness rather than distance. In a relationship, it is the quality that allows us to be fully known — including in our worst and most broken moments — and still loved. It is what makes a marriage a sanctuary rather than just a shared address.

Most of us are far harsher judges of our partners than we would be of strangers in identical circumstances. If a colleague at work makes a mistake, we are usually generous: they must have been under pressure, they didn't mean it, everyone slips sometimes. If our partner makes the same mistake, the harsh inner voice is quick to say: how could they, why always this, will they ever learn? We extend compassion outward readily and withhold it from the person closest to us.

This is a habit worth examining. Your partner is not a project to be fixed, a collection of flaws to be cataloged and corrected. They are a human being doing their best — just as you are — in the face of pressures, fears, and limitations that you may not always fully see. Compassion means holding that awareness, especially in moments of frustration.

Compassion does something deeper than easing tension — it creates emotional safety. When a person knows that their pain will be met with kindness rather than criticism, they begin to open up rather than protect. They share more honestly. They trust more fully. Over time, this kind of response builds a foundation in which both partners feel safe enough to be imperfect, which is essential in any lasting relationship.

There is also an important distinction that compassion brings into a marriage: the difference between reaction and response. Reaction is immediate, often driven by ego, frustration, or misunderstanding. Response is intentional. It creates space between what happens and how you choose to engage with it. Compassion lives in that space. It allows you to pause, to consider, and to meet your partner in a way that strengthens the relationship rather than strains it.

It also means responding to your partner's pain with presence rather than problem-solving. We often reach for solutions when our partner simply needs to be heard. Learning to ask, "Do you want me to help you think through this, or do you just need me to listen?" is one of the most compassionate things a partner can do.

Compassion also extends to your partner's history. Every person carries wounds from before you. Patterns of behavior that frustrate you — defensiveness, avoidance, difficulty with trust — almost always have roots in experiences that preceded your relationship. This does not excuse hurtful behavior. But it provides a lens through which frustration can, with practice, transform into something more like understanding.

Sometimes compassion means helping. Sometimes it means listening. Sometimes it means simply staying close when there is nothing to fix.

Marriage becomes a refuge when compassion is stronger than criticism.

QUICK REMINDERS

- Your spouse is not your project.
- Pain often hides beneath irritation.
- Kindness in difficult moments creates deep safety.

ASK YOURSELVES

When my spouse is struggling, do they experience me as a source of pressure or comfort?

LITTLE TRUTH TO KEEP

Compassion turns a house into a shelter.

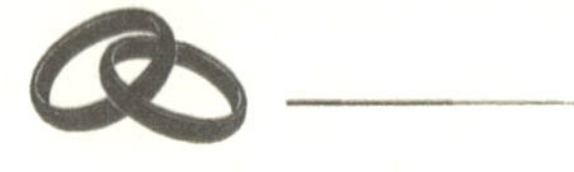

6.

Compromise

Both people matter

Compromise is the art of making room for two lives inside one marriage.

It is not surrender. It is not the erasure of your own needs in service of your partner's. That is not compromise — that is self-abandonment, and it breeds resentment with remarkable efficiency. True compromise is the collaborative negotiation between two people who both matter; both have needs, and both understand that a shared life requires the constant, creative work of finding arrangements that honor them both as fully as possible.

Early in our marriage, I remember one holiday conversation that was not really about the holiday at all. We were deciding where to spend the day, and both of us had good reasons for our choices. I came into the conversation thinking mainly about tradition and convenience. Lorie was thinking about people, obligations, and how the day would actually feel once we were in it.

At first, I treated the conversation as if one of us would naturally be proven right. But as we talked, it became clear that neither of us was asking for something unreasonable. We were simply seeing the day through different lenses. What changed the conversation was not that one of us gave in. It was that we both began to make room for the other person's point of view.

That is often what compromise looks like in a marriage — not losing, not yielding under pressure, but widening the space until both people can fit inside the decision.

This sounds simple. It is not. We are remarkably good at disguising preferences as needs, at elevating the things we merely want into non-negotiables that our partner must simply accept. The spouse who insists on spending every holiday with their family of origin and presents this as non-negotiable may be protecting something genuinely important — or may simply be accustomed to getting their way. Learning the difference and being honest about it, is a prerequisite to genuine compromise.

Strong couples understand that marriage is not a contest with one winner. It is a creative negotiation that respects both people.

There is another layer to compromise that matters just as much: the willingness to be influenced. Many disagreements in marriage do not become destructive because the issue itself is so large, but because one or both people resist letting the other person's perspective affect them. Healthy compromise begins when a spouse can say, in effect, "Your point of view matters enough to shape my own." Research on long-term relationships has repeatedly shown that couples do better when both partners accept each other's influence rather than treating every disagreement like a power struggle.

Compromise also requires reciprocity over time. If one partner is always the one making concessions, that is not a compromise. It is a power imbalance. Thriving couples maintain a general sense of equity, making sure the account of whose needs took priority does not get too lopsided.

That sense of fairness does not mean everything is split evenly in every moment. Life does not work that way. One season may require more from one spouse; another season may ask more of the other. What matters is the larger pattern. When both people feel that their needs are taken seriously and that sacrifices are recognized rather than assumed, compromise strengthens the relationship instead of weakening it. Research on supportive relationships consistently finds that people are most satisfied when the relationship feels broadly equitable and reciprocal over time.

Healthy compromise leaves both people feeling heard, even when neither gets everything.

The goal is not my way or your way. The goal is a wise way forward for us.

QUICK REMINDERS

- Not every want is a need.
- Fairness matters over the long haul.
- Good compromise protects the relationship without erasing the individual.

ASK YOURSELVES

Are we trying to win, or are we trying to build something that honors both of us?

LITTLE TRUTH TO KEEP

The best compromises do not create losers. They create a partnership.

7. Concern

Notice what matters to your spouse

Concern is the quality of paying attention to your partner's well-being with the same investment you bring to your own. Not surveillance — not anxious monitoring that leaves no room for the other person to have a private inner life — but a genuine, steady interest in how your partner is doing, in the fullest sense: emotionally, physically, professionally, spiritually.

It means noticing the changes before they become crises. It means asking "How are you really doing?" with the intention of actually hearing the answer, rather than as a social courtesy. It means being the kind of partner whose care is tangible enough that your partner never feels they are carrying something difficult alone.

The longer you are married, the more you notice the subtle signals when something is off with your spouse. That has happened many times over the years in my marriage to Lorie. In those moments, I could sense something wasn't right, but nothing had been said. There was no clear reason, no specific event to point to — just a difference in her tone, a quietness that didn't belong to her usual rhythm.

It can be convenient to ignore it, because nothing appears wrong on the surface. But over time, I've learned that those small signals often matter most. So instead of moving past it, I ask a simple question — not just "How are you?" but "What's really going on?"

At first, she may hesitate to share, or the answer might be brief. But as we keep talking, more usually comes out — not something dramatic, but something real. And what strikes me afterward is how easily that moment could have been missed, how quickly life can move past something important if I don't take the time to stop and notice.

Lorie does the same thing with me. She knows me like a book. She picks up on my moods and subtle shifts in temperament and seems to know exactly when to gently ask — out of concern — what's bothering me.

That is what concern does. It slows things down long enough for what matters to be seen.

Concern is the antidote to the particular loneliness that can develop inside a long-term relationship — the loneliness of feeling invisible to the person who should know you best. Two people can live in the same home, share the same bed, and still feel unseen. Concern helps prevent that loneliness. It communicates: your inner life matters to me.

There is also a deeper truth about concern that often goes unspoken: it creates emotional security. When a person knows that someone is paying attention — not in a controlling way, but in a steady, caring way — they feel held within the relationship. They do not have to carry everything alone. People feel most connected in relationships where they experience responsiveness — where their partner notices, responds, and engages with their emotional world. Concern is one of the clearest expressions of that responsiveness.

Concern also operates in small, ongoing moments, not just in times of stress. It shows up in remembering what is coming up in your partner's day, checking in after something important, and noticing shifts in mood before they are explained. Over time, these small acts form a pattern. And that pattern sends a powerful message: you are not alone in your life — I am paying attention to it with you.

It is also the quality that carries a relationship through the difficult passages of life. Illness, loss, career setbacks, the death of parents, the emptying of a nest — all of these test a partnership. The couples who move through them most gracefully are those who have developed the habit of showing concern for each other before a crisis arises. By the time the challenging thing comes, the muscle is already developed.

In a long marriage, concern takes on a particular quality. You have watched each other long enough to know the early signs — the particular silence that means something is wrong, the way they carry themselves when they are carrying too much, the forced cheerfulness that signals the opposite of cheer.

That deep literacy of a person, accumulated over years, is one of marriage's most intimate gifts. It allows you to reach for someone before they have to reach out. To say I see it before they have to say I need help. That kind of concern cannot be manufactured. It is built slowly, through the sustained practice of paying attention.

Love deepens when one person notices before the other has to cry out for attention.

QUICK REMINDERS

- Watch gently, not anxiously.
- Noticing is one of love's purest forms.
- The question "What's going on?" can change everything.

ASK YOURSELVES

Does my spouse feel that I pay attention to their well-being, or only to my own concerns?

LITTLE TRUTH TO KEEP

Being noticed is one of the sweetest forms of being loved.

8.

Conciliation

Learn how to come back together

Conciliation is the art of de-escalation, of the gesture or the word that opens the door back to connection after conflict has pushed you to opposite sides of the room. It is the willingness to value the relationship above the satisfaction of winning the argument, the comfort of righteous anger, or the protective distance of a cold silence.

Conciliation is the move back toward peace.

Over the course of 52 years of marriage, as you would expect, there have been many occasions when Lorie and I were clearly at odds — in most cases not over anything particularly significant, but enough to create distance. The conversation had ended, but the feeling hadn't. We were moving around each other rather than with each other, both holding onto our positions, neither quite ready to let go.

At some point, we always realize that nothing is actually being solved by the distance. The silence isn't productive. It doesn't help or heal anything — it simply extends the moment. So one of us will finally make a small move — not a full resolution, not an explanation, just a simple step back toward the other person. A comment, a tone shift, something that says, "I don't want this distance to continue."

It doesn't always fix everything instantly, of course. But it changes the direction of the conflict. And often, that's all conciliation needs to do — not resolve the issue completely, but reopen the connection.

What makes conciliation difficult is that it usually requires one person to go first — to extend the olive branch before the argument is fully resolved, before the hurt is fully processed, before the other person has shown any sign of meeting you halfway. That takes courage. It takes the secure knowledge that your own dignity does not depend on the other person yielding before you do.

There is also a timing element to conciliation that is often overlooked. Trying to repair too quickly, before emotions have even slightly settled, can feel dismissive or insincere. Waiting too long allows the distance to harden. The skill is in sensing when the moment is right — when enough space has been created to allow a softer approach, but not so much time that disconnection becomes comfortable. That awareness develops over time and becomes one of the quiet strengths of a mature relationship.

Conciliation is the skill of repair. It takes many forms. Sometimes it is an apology — a genuine one, not the defensive pseudo-apology ("I'm sorry you felt that way"), but the real thing: "I was wrong. I shouldn't have said that. I'm sorry." Sometimes it is a touch — a hand on a shoulder, a willingness to be physically present after emotional distance has opened up. Sometimes it is simply the acknowledgment that both of you want to get unstuck, that neither of you wants to spend the evening this way.

Another truth about conciliation is that it is often less about words than about tone and posture. A softened voice, a willingness to sit closer, an openness in body language — these signals can communicate "I'm ready to reconnect" long before the right words are found.

In many cases, the repair begins not with what is said, but with how it is said.

It also takes the ability to hold two things simultaneously: the legitimate grievance you may still have and the deeper commitment to your partner that transcends the immediate dispute. You can be hurt and still be kind. You can be angry and still be generous. Conciliation is not the erasure of grievance. It is the decision that the grievance can be addressed differently, more gently, after the heat has lowered.

What prevents most couples from conciliating quickly is pride — the quiet, powerful conviction that whoever moves first has somehow lost. This is one of the most expensive misunderstandings in marriage.

In reality, the partner who extends the first olive branch has not surrendered. They have demonstrated something far more valuable: that they love this person more than they love being right.

Over the course of a long marriage, I have found that the moments I reached out first — before I felt ready, before the argument was resolved, before I was certain of a warm reception — were often the ones that built the most trust. Not because I gave in. But because I showed that the relationship mattered more to me than the last word.

A marriage grows stronger when both people learn that conflict does not have to be the end of a connection.

QUICK REMINDERS

- Repair matters more than being right.
- A soft answer can end a hard evening.
- Someone must be willing to go first.

ASK YOURSELVES

How quickly do we repair after a conflict, and what makes repair harder than it needs to be?

LITTLE TRUTH TO KEEP

Strong couples do not avoid conflict. They learn how to return from it.

9.

Courtesy

Don't save your worst for the one you love most

Courtesy is simple respect, expressed daily.

Too many people are more polite to strangers than they are to their own husband or wife. They are pleasant and kind at the grocery store, in meetings, at restaurants, and on the phone, then come home and let sharpness spill freely.

Over the years in our marriage, there have been many times when I've said something to Lorie in a tone I would never have used with anyone else. It wasn't what I said — it was how I said it. Quick. Dismissive. Slightly impatient. And the moment it left my mouth, I knew it. I felt it immediately.

If I had been speaking to a colleague, a neighbor, or even a stranger, I would have chosen my words more carefully. I would have softened the tone. I would have been more aware. But familiarity had made me careless.

That realization stayed with me, because it raised a question I couldn't ignore: why would I offer more courtesy to people who matter less to me than to the person who matters most?

The truth is, it's easy to let your guard down at home. The place that should feel safest can also become the place where we are least filtered, least thoughtful, and least aware of how we come across. But over time, those moments matter. Tone accumulates. A pattern forms. And what begins as occasional carelessness can slowly shape how the relationship feels day to day.

That is why courtesy matters more than it seems. It is not about perfection. It is about awareness. It is about choosing, even in ordinary moments, to speak with the same respect you would offer anyone else — and especially the person you love most.

Courtesy in a relationship is not formality. It helps keep love from growing coarse. It is not stiffness or the suppression of honesty in favor of pleasantness. It is, at its core, the simple practice of treating your partner with the respect and consideration they deserve — and that the relationship requires in order to remain a place of comfort rather than tension.

There is a deeper reason courtesy matters as much as it does: tone and respect shape the emotional climate of a relationship over time. Research on long-term marriages consistently shows that patterns of criticism, defensiveness, and especially contempt — even in small, repeated moments — are among the strongest predictors of relationship breakdown. Courtesy acts as a daily safeguard against those patterns. It keeps disagreements from turning personal and prevents irritation from hardening into something more corrosive.

It is saying “please” and “thank you”. It is watching your tone. It is not interrupting, belittling, dismissing, or speaking carelessly — especially in front of others — simply because your spouse is familiar and always there.

Courtesy also means being careful with humor. The line between playful teasing and cutting sarcasm is not always clear, and it shifts depending on the day, the mood, and the accumulated history of similar remarks. Couples who use humor well can defuse tension and bring lightness to difficulty. Couples who rely on sarcasm as their default register often find that what reads as funny to them reads as contempt to their partner. Contempt — the sense that one partner feels fundamentally superior to the other — is the single strongest predictor of relationship failure.

Another important truth is that courtesy is cumulative. A single sharp comment may pass quickly, but repeated over time, small moments of disrespect begin to define the tone of the relationship. In the same way, small, consistent acts of courtesy build a quiet but powerful sense of safety. A respectful tone, a thoughtful response, a moment of restraint — these are not dramatic gestures, but they shape how it feels to live together day after day.

Your partner deserves to be treated as a person worthy of basic dignity. That is courtesy. And in long-term relationships, where the extraordinary has given way to the ordinary, courtesy is the daily practice that keeps the ordinary from sliding into contempt.

Familiarity should deepen tenderness, not weaken basic decency.

QUICK REMINDERS

- Tone is part of love.
- Respect is not reserved for public settings.
- What feels small to you may feel cutting to your spouse.

ASK YOURSELVES

Would I speak to a stranger the way I sometimes speak to my spouse?

LITTLE TRUTH TO KEEP

Courtesy keeps ordinary love from turning rough.

10.

Cooperation

Act like a team

Cooperation is a shared effort in a shared life.

It is the practice of functioning as a genuine team — sharing the labor in ways that draw on each partner's strengths and honor each partner's limitations. It means not keeping score in the punitive sense, but maintaining a general sense of equity: both partners carrying their weight in the shared enterprise of the household, the family, the finances, the social calendar, and the emotional maintenance of the relationship itself.

I remember a season in our marriage when the pace of life picked up — work demands, family responsibilities, and everything that comes with raising a young family. Like many couples, we divided things up in ways that felt natural at the time. I focused on certain responsibilities, Lorie on others. On the surface, it seemed to work.

But over time, I began to realize there was far more happening than I was aware of. There were things being managed, anticipated, and handled that never showed up on any list — things that simply got done because Lorie carried them. I wasn't ignoring them. I just wasn't seeing them. And she carried most of that load without complaint — or at least without many complaints, though the occasional one would land just enough to get my attention and prompt me to help... for a while.

It's not that I didn't understand. It's that I slipped back into old habits. And that's what I've come to see over time: cooperation isn't just about doing your share of what's visible. It's about becoming aware of what isn't visible — and consistently stepping into it.

For much of our marriage, the division of responsibilities at home followed a fairly traditional pattern. Lorie carried the bulk of the household load — shopping, cooking, cleaning, laundry, getting the kids ready for school, and countless other details that come with running a home. My contributions, by comparison, were lighter and more occasional. At the time, it didn't feel unusual. It was simply how things were done, and I didn't question it nearly enough.

Over time, as Lorie spoke up more about the imbalance, I began to see it differently. I started to take on more — slowly at first, and then more intentionally. I have improved, without question, but the truth is, she has still carried more than her share. Even now, we joke about it. I'll say I've taken on cooking, and she'll quickly clarify that it means I make dinner about once a month and handle the dishwasher and the pots. There's humor in it, but also truth. Like many husbands, I have fallen short in this area. I'm better than I was, but I still have room — and responsibility — to do more.

That awareness — and the willingness to keep adjusting — is what cooperation asks of both people over time.

Cooperation requires visibility. Both partners need to see the full scope of what a shared life requires — not just the tasks they already do, but also the ones they don't notice because someone else has always managed them. Asking, "What needs to happen that

I'm not currently aware of?" is a surprisingly productive question for any partnership.

There is a deeper layer to this that many couples overlook: the "mental load." In many relationships, one partner quietly carries the responsibility of tracking what needs to be done — remembering appointments, anticipating needs, managing details before they become problems. This invisible labor can be just as taxing as physical tasks, and often more so, because it is continuous and largely unrecognized. True cooperation requires not just helping when asked, but sharing in that awareness so that the burden is not carried alone.

But cooperation is not only about chores and logistics. It is also about navigating life's larger challenges together — financial decisions, parenting, the care of aging parents, the ongoing negotiation of two careers and two sets of needs. These require the same spirit of teamwork: we are in this together. Your success is my success. Your burden is my burden.

Another important dimension of cooperation is alignment in mindset. Strong couples approach challenges with a shared orientation: it is not me versus you — it is us versus the problem. That shift may sound small, but it changes everything. It reduces defensiveness, lowers tension, and opens the door to collaborative problem-solving. When both people are on the same side, solutions become easier to find because the goal is no longer to win, but to move forward together.

A marriage weakens when one person becomes the default carrier of everything unseen and unglamorous. Dishes are not the whole story. There are countless invisible tasks that can leave one person depleted while the other remains unaware.

Cooperation is also emotional. It means facing challenges together instead of assigning blame from opposite corners. It means solving problems as partners, not prosecutors.

The happiest marriages sound less like "That's your problem" and more like "How do we handle this together?"

QUICK REMINDERS

- Teamwork must include invisible labor, too.
- A shared life requires shared responsibility.
- Resentment grows where effort stays unequal for too long.

ASK YOURSELVES

Are we functioning like true partners, or has one of us quietly become the default manager of everything?

LITTLE TRUTH TO KEEP

Marriage feels lighter when the load is truly shared.

11.

Caring

Let affection stay active

Caring is warm, ongoing, visible love.

It is being actively interested in your partner's experience — an interest that permeates the texture of daily life. It is distinct from concern, which watches over well-being, in that it is less watchful and more simply warm: genuine affection expressed in the continuous small ways that constitute the emotional fabric of a relationship.

I remember a period in our marriage when life felt especially full — work, responsibilities, schedules, and all the demands that come with raising a family and building a life together. Nothing was wrong, but something subtle had shifted. We were efficient. We were managing everything that needed to be managed. But we weren't always expressing the warmth that had once come more naturally.

There was a moment when that became clear to me — not through anything dramatic, but through its absence. I realized that days could go by where we were functioning well together, but not actively showing affection. We were connected in responsibility, but not always in warmth.

That awareness changed something for me. Caring isn't just something you feel. It's something you express. And if it isn't expressed, over time, it can begin to feel like it isn't there — even when it is.

Caring is the morning coffee made without being asked. The text sent at two in the afternoon just to say you were thinking about them. The back rub after an exhausting day, the check-in when they seem low, the laughter shared at nothing in particular because you are simply glad to be in the same room together.

It is the physical expression of affection that does not require special occasions — the hand held during a walk, the touch on the shoulder in passing, the look across a crowded room that says, *I see you, and I'm glad you're mine*. The nightly kiss before bed, accompanied by a sincere "I love you."

There is a deeper truth about caring that often goes unrecognized: it is one of the primary ways emotional connection is maintained over time. Research on long-term relationships shows that couples who regularly express small moments of affection and responsiveness — brief check-ins, shared humor, physical touch, simple acknowledgments — maintain stronger emotional bonds than those who rely only on occasional grand gestures. These moments may seem minor, but they accumulate. They form the day-to-day experience of being loved.

Caring also requires intentionality. Affection does not always sustain itself automatically over time. As life becomes more complex, warmth can be crowded out by responsibility unless it is protected. The strongest couples are not necessarily the ones who feel more love — they are the ones who continue to express it, even when they are busy, tired, or distracted. They understand that caring is not something to be taken for granted. It is something to be demonstrated.

Caring also means actively tending to your partner's flourishing — not just their survival, not just their basic needs, but their becoming. Are they pursuing what matters to them? Are they growing? Are there ways you can support that? A caring partner celebrates their spouse's achievements with genuine gladness, not manufactured enthusiasm.

It also means caring for the relationship itself – treating it as a living thing that requires tending. Relationships don't maintain themselves. They require the ongoing investment of time, attention, affection, and intentionality. The couple who protect time for genuine connection, who refuse to let the relationship be indefinitely crowded out by the logistical demands of a busy life, is doing the work of caring for the relationship as a relationship, not just managing a shared enterprise.

The opposite of caring in a relationship is not hate. It is indifference – the gradual erosion of interest in your partner as a person, the slide from seeing them to merely coexisting with them. Indifference is far more dangerous than conflict because it does not announce itself. It arrives quietly, disguised as busyness, fatigue, or the comfortable habit of not having to try anymore.

It is easy for couples to become efficient partners without remaining affectionate partners. They manage the household, pay the bills, and coordinate the calendar, but they forget to nurture warmth. Caring helps protect against emotional drift. It reminds both people that they are not merely running a life. They are still loving one another in it.

QUICK REMINDERS

- Warmth should not disappear into routine.
- Small affection often matters more than grand gestures.
- Indifference is more dangerous than inconvenience.

ASK YOURSELVES

How does my spouse experience my affection on an ordinary day?

LITTLE TRUTH TO KEEP

The small signs of love are often the strongest.

12.

Companionship

Actually enjoy being together

Companionship is one of marriage's quiet treasures.

It is the quality of the relationship that shows up not in the dramatic moments, but in the ordinary ones — the unhurried Saturday morning, the evening walk, the comfortable silence over dinner, the shared amusement at the news, the years and years of simply being together and finding that enough.

When people ask me about our long marriage and what the secret is, I usually tell them two simple things that have always worked for Lorie and me: we make each other laugh every day, and we are each other's best friend. We genuinely enjoy being together.

That may sound natural — and in many ways it is — but it still requires something from both of us. It requires presence. It requires being mindful of the time we share. Companionship doesn't sustain itself automatically.

I remember a stretch of time, years into our marriage, when life had settled into a rhythm. The urgency of the early years had passed. The demands were still there, but they were different. And what stood out to me in that season was how much I genuinely enjoyed just being with Lorie.

There didn't have to be a plan. No special occasion. We could sit and talk, or not talk. Take a walk, watch something together, or simply share the same space at the end of the day. And in those moments, I realized something that doesn't get talked about enough: the ability to simply enjoy each other's company is not automatic. It's something that develops — and something that needs to be protected.

Companionship is the quality that the early, urgent intensity of romantic love often obscures, and that only fully reveals itself in the settled intimacy of a long partnership. Research consistently shows that one of the strongest predictors of long-term relationship satisfaction is the quality of friendship between partners. Not passion — friendship. The sense that this person is someone you genuinely like, whose company you genuinely enjoy, who you would choose to spend time with even if there were no romantic or practical tie binding you together.

There is also growing recognition that shared positive experiences — even small ones — play a central role in sustaining companionship. Couples who regularly engage in simple, enjoyable activities together tend to maintain stronger emotional bonds over time. These shared moments create a reservoir of goodwill and connection that carries the relationship through more difficult periods. It is not the scale of the experience that matters, but the consistency of it.

This is worth pausing on, because it cuts against the dominant cultural narrative of what makes a relationship valuable. We hear a lot about chemistry, passion, attraction, and desire. We hear less about the quiet gift of someone you can simply be with — without performance, without agenda, without having to be anything other than exactly who you are on an ordinary day.

Companionship requires the protection of time. It requires the deliberate carving out of hours that are not for tasks or productivity, but simply for being together. A walk with no destination. A meal cooked together spontaneously. A film watched on the sofa, feet tangled together, without looking at your phone.

Another important dimension of companionship is presence. It is possible to be physically together and mentally elsewhere – distracted, preoccupied, partially engaged, glued to our phones. True companionship requires attention. It is the willingness to be fully there with the other person, even in small moments. That kind of presence communicates something powerful: not just that you are together, but that you are choosing to be together in that moment.

It also requires genuine curiosity about each other – not the interrogative curiosity of a job interview, but the ongoing, delighted interest in who this person is and is becoming. What are they reading? What are they thinking about? What surprised them today? The couples who remain genuinely curious about each other after thirty years tend to report the highest levels of satisfaction, because curiosity keeps companionship alive in the face of familiarity.

A rich marriage is not only built on duty. It is built on delight in each other's company.

QUICK REMINDERS

- Friendship is a primary building block in a marriage.
- Time together must be protected, not assumed.
- Curiosity keeps love alive for the long haul.

ASK YOURSELVES

Do we still make space to enjoy one another apart from tasks and responsibilities?

LITTLE TRUTH TO KEEP

It is a gift to be married to someone you still genuinely like to spend time with.

13.

Candor

Tell the truth with love

Candor is honest speech offered with care.

Many spouses avoid the truth because they fear conflict, disappointment, or discomfort. They say less than they mean. They hide hurt. They withhold doubts. They soften reality until the relationship contains politeness, but not full honesty.

I can think of times in our marriage when I chose the easier path instead of the honest one. Not because I intended to deceive, but because I wanted to avoid a difficult conversation or protect Lorie from something I thought might upset her. It felt harmless in the moment — even considerate. But over time, I came to see that withholding truth, even gently, creates distance.

Lorie has called me out on that at times, especially when she sensed I wasn't sharing something she should know. Finances have been one example. There were times when I spent money without telling her because I suspected she wouldn't be pleased. I told myself I wasn't being dishonest – but choosing not to share something your partner has a right to know is its own form of avoidance.

In those moments, the conversation may be avoided, but the connection is not strengthened. What remains unsaid carries weight. I've learned it is far better to speak honestly – even when it's uncomfortable – than to allow silence or partial truth to slowly reshape the relationship. Because over time, that erodes trust, which is one of the essential pillars of a marriage.

Candor is critically important in every marriage. Even when honesty is uncomfortable, even when it risks conflict, even when it would be easier to say what the other person wants to hear, candor should be the rule. It is the courage to trust your partner enough to give them reality rather than a curated version of it.There is a deeper reason candor matters as much as it does: it builds trust in a way nothing else can. Research consistently shows that trust is strengthened not simply by positive interactions, but by the reliability of what is shared. When partners know that what they are hearing is real — not edited, not managed — it creates a sense of security that allows the relationship to deepen. Without that, even kind relationships can feel uncertain beneath the surface.

Do not mistake candor for cruelty. The person who delivers hard truths without regard for how they land — who mistakes bluntness for honesty and harshness for integrity — has confused two very different things. Candor is not the license to say whatever you feel whenever you feel it. It is the disciplined practice of saying what is true in ways that can actually be heard — with care, with timing, and with the clear intention that honesty comes from love rather than frustration.

Another important dimension of candor is psychological safety — the shared understanding that truth can be spoken without fear of disproportionate reaction or lasting damage. In strong relationships, both partners learn not only how to speak honestly, but how to receive honesty. That means listening without immediate defensiveness, resisting the urge to retaliate, and recognizing that even difficult truths are being offered in service of the relationship.

Candor thrives where both people feel safe telling and hearing the truth.

In a healthy marriage, honesty shows up in very practical ways: the willingness to say, "I'm not fine." The courage to name something that has been sitting between you for weeks. The ability to acknowledge your own fault in a conflict rather than building a case for your defense.

Candor becomes even more important over time, because long-term relationships create a natural temptation to manage each other — to protect feelings, shape reactions, or avoid discomfort by controlling what is shared. But when we do that, we don't just avoid conflict — we limit how fully we are known.

A relationship in which candor flourishes is one in which both partners can trust what they are told. The knowledge that your partner speaks honestly with you — that their reassurances are real and not managed, that their enthusiasm is genuine — creates a level of security that cannot be built any other way.

Truth, kindly spoken, is one of love's greatest gifts.

QUICK REMINDERS

- Honesty builds safety when it is delivered with care.
- Hidden truth creates hidden distance.
- Candor is how love stays real.

ASK YOURSELVES

What have I been editing, minimizing, or avoiding instead of saying honestly and lovingly?

LITTLE TRUTH TO KEEP

Intimacy cannot thrive where truth is rationed.

14.

Courage

Be brave enough to protect the marriage

Courage in marriage is rarely dramatic.

It is not about heroics. It is about the small, daily acts of bravery that authentic intimacy requires — saying the difficult thing, having the overdue conversation, and addressing the pattern that has gone unaddressed for too long. It is about choosing the discomfort of honesty over the comfort of avoidance, the exposure of genuine vulnerability over the safety of self-protection.

I can think of times in our marriage when I knew there was something that needed to be said — something uncomfortable, something that carried the risk of tension or misunderstanding. And like most people, my instinct wasn't to move toward it. It was to delay, to soften it, to hope it might resolve itself without having to be addressed directly.

But what I've learned over time is that those are often the moments that matter most. The conversation you hesitate to have is usually the one that has the greatest potential to strengthen the relationship – if you have the courage to engage it with honesty and care.

It takes courage to be the first one to apologize. It takes courage to admit that you have been wrong – not simply wrong about a fact, but wrong in how you treated your partner, wrong in the habits and assumptions that have calcified over the years. It takes courage to say, "I am afraid," or "I need something I haven't been getting," or "I am not happy, and I want us to fix it."

There is a deeper dimension to courage in relationships that is often overlooked: the willingness to be vulnerable. Research consistently shows that vulnerability – the ability to be open about fears, needs, and imperfections – is one of the strongest drivers of emotional connection. And yet it is also one of the hardest things to practice, because it requires lowering the very defenses we rely on to protect ourselves. Courage is what allows that to happen.

Courage also means facing issues early rather than allowing them to harden over time. Avoidance may reduce discomfort in the short term, but it almost always increases it in the long term. Small issues left unspoken tend to grow – not necessarily in size, but in weight. They accumulate, they distort perception, and they quietly reshape the tone of a relationship. Courage interrupts that pattern by bringing things into the open while they are still manageable.

Having courage in a marriage means being willing to seek help. The couples who go to therapy are often the ones brave enough to say: We cannot figure this out alone, and we care enough about this relationship to ask for help. Far too many couples avoid this step until it is too late, because asking for help feels like an admission of failure. It is not. It is an act of courage – and of love.

In a culture that normalizes the exit – which treats leaving as freedom and staying as limitation – choosing to remain in a difficult but repairable relationship and do the work it requires is a form of courage. Not every relationship should be saved. But many that end should have been fought for more, and weren't, because the effort required a level of courage that was just out of reach.

Lastly, courage means being willing to let yourself be changed. Genuine intimacy – the kind that deepens over decades – requires the willingness to be affected by the person you love, to allow their experience to genuinely impact your own, to update your understanding of yourself through the mirror of their knowledge of you. That requires the courage to be seen, which is quite different from merely being looked at.

The marriage you want often lies on the other side of the conversation you are afraid to have.

QUICK REMINDERS

- Avoidance has a cost.
- Vulnerability is not weakness.
- Asking for help can be an act of love.

ASK YOURSELVES

What brave conversation would strengthen our marriage if we finally had it?

LITTLE TRUTH TO KEEP

Marriage grows when fear no longer runs the room.

15. Celebration

Notice what is good

Celebration is intentional gratitude within the marriage.

It is the conscious, deliberate recognition of what is right in your relationship and your life together. It is the counterweight to the human tendency — deeply wired and extensively documented — to notice what is wrong far more readily than what is right. In a relationship, this means we are more likely to catalog the disappointments than to genuinely register the joys. We remember the arguments. We forget the laughter and the good times. Celebration is the intentional correction of that imbalance.

As I reflect on the years of our marriage, I can recall moments — not tied to any particular milestone — when I paused to look at the life Lorie and I had built together. Nothing dramatic was happening, just ordinary days. But something about those moments made me step back and see them differently — the years behind us, the shared experiences, the challenges we had navigated, and the quiet routines that now define our lives.

What struck me most was how easy it would have been to overlook it all — to keep moving forward without ever fully recognizing what was already there. Those moments have stayed with me because they remind me that appreciation doesn't happen automatically. It has to be chosen.

Celebration takes many forms. The most obvious is the marking of milestones: anniversaries, birthdays, achievements, the calendar events that most couples already recognize. But the couples who truly cultivate celebration go far beyond the calendar. They celebrate the ordinary. They acknowledge the everyday gifts of the relationship — the person who always knows how to make you laugh, the partner who sat with you through a hard night, the shared morning coffee. Named and celebrated, these small things become a story you are consciously writing together.

There is also a deeper psychological truth behind this: what we consistently notice begins to shape how we experience the relationship itself. Research in relationships shows that couples who intentionally focus on positive moments — even small ones — tend to build stronger emotional bonds and greater overall satisfaction. Not because they ignore problems, but because they refuse to let problems define the entire narrative. Celebration helps anchor the relationship in what is working, not just what needs attention.

Celebration also means celebrating each other as individuals — not just the relationship, but the person. When your partner achieves something, when they grow, when they do something you admire, say so. Genuinely. One of the loneliest things in a long marriage can be the sense that your partner has long since stopped being surprised or impressed by you — that they have you fully cataloged and filed. A genuine celebration of each other's ongoing development communicates something vital: I am still paying attention. You still have the capacity to amaze and delight me.

Another important dimension of celebration is responsiveness — how we react to each other's good news. Studies have shown that couples who actively and positively respond to each other's successes (not just passively or briefly) strengthen trust and connection. A simple moment — sharing something good that happened — becomes an opportunity to reinforce the bond when it is met with enthusiasm, interest, and genuine joy.

Celebration is also the practice of gratitude, made audible. Research on gratitude consistently shows that couples who regularly express genuine appreciation for each other report higher satisfaction, deeper connection, and greater resilience in the face of difficulty. This is not because gratitude is magic. It is because expressed gratitude shifts both the giver and the receiver toward what is present and good rather than toward what is absent and disappointing.

There is something to be said for occasionally stepping back from the daily demands of a relationship and saying: Look at what we have built. Look at how far we have come. Look at the life we have made together. This kind of reflective celebration is not nostalgia. It is the forward-looking recognition of people who, with clarity and gratitude, understand what they have.

QUICK REMINDERS

- Do not save appreciation for special occasions.
- Gratitude should be spoken, not merely felt.
- A marriage grows warmer when goodness is named.

ASK YOURSELVES

What have I come to take for granted that I should start appreciating aloud again?

LITTLE TRUTH TO KEEP

A grateful marriage is often a happier marriage.

16.

Consistency

The small things, done again and again

Consistency is what turns every other C from an idea into a way of life.

Real love is not a performance. Real love is a practice. And a practice is defined by its consistency — by what you do not just when it matters most, but when it matters least; not just when you feel inspired, but when you feel tired, distracted, and entirely disinclined to be your best self.

Throughout the past 52 years, I've come to see that the strength of our marriage has far less to do with any single moment and far more to do with what we did repeatedly. Not the big decisions, but the small, daily choices — how we spoke to each other, how we showed up, how we handled ordinary moments that no one else ever saw.

It's easy to think that what matters most are the defining conversations or the turning points. And those moments do matter. But what shapes a marriage far more is what happens in between — the patterns that quietly form through repetition.

The power of consistency is cumulative in ways that are difficult to see in the moment but impossible to miss over time. Couples who have been consistently kind to each other are surrounded, after twenty years, by a deep well of goodwill and positive history that insulates them against the inevitable difficulties. Couples who have been consistently careless — not cruel, just careless, just absent, just not paying attention — find, after twenty years, that the well is dry and there is nothing left to draw on when they need it.

There is a deeper reason for this: patterns of behavior become the emotional climate of a relationship. Research consistently shows that it is not isolated actions that define relationship satisfaction, but repeated interactions over time. A kind word once is meaningful. A kind pattern becomes identity.

Consistency is what allows trust, safety, and affection to take root and endure.

Consistency is the goodnight kiss. The daily check-in. The steady respect. The recurring apology. The habit of telling the truth. The dependable kindness that shows up not only in milestone moments, but on random, ordinary days.

It is the expressed appreciation for ordinary acts — the dinner made, the errand run, the call returned — that might otherwise be taken for granted. It is the choosing, day after day, to be the kind of partner you committed to being on the best day of your life, even on the days that feel like the opposite.

Another important dimension of consistency is reliability. In strong relationships, partners come to trust not just what is said, but what can be expected. Reliability builds a quiet form of confidence: I know who you are going to be tomorrow, and I can depend on it. That kind of steadiness is deeply reassuring, and often far more powerful than occasional grand gestures.

Over time, marriages create an emotional account. Every warm moment is a deposit. Every careless dismissal is a withdrawal. The balance is not obvious day by day, but over the years it becomes unmistakable. Consistency fills the account with trust, affection, goodwill, and safety.

Without consistency, even beautiful intentions stay temporary.

Love does not become strong because it is occasionally profound. It becomes strong because it is reliably practiced.

QUICK REMINDERS

- What you repeat becomes your marriage.
- Small habits shape long outcomes.
- Reliability is romantic in ways people often underestimate.

ASK YOURSELVES

What one loving habit, practiced consistently, would most strengthen our marriage right now?

LITTLE TRUTH TO KEEP

Real love is not a performance. Real love is a practice.

Closing Thoughts

Start with one.

Sixteen qualities may sound like a lot. So do not begin with all sixteen. Begin with one.

Choose the C your marriage needs most right now. Maybe you need better communication. Maybe you need more courtesy. Maybe you need more celebration, more candor, more concern, or more consistency.

Pick one. Practice it on purpose. Let it become visible in the way you speak, listen, respond, and show up.

Then choose another.

A happy marriage is not built in one giant leap. It is built one decision, one kindness, one repair, one truth, one act of love at a time.

After more than fifty years of marriage, this is what I believe most deeply:

Not that strong marriages are perfect.

Not that they avoid pain.

Not that they never fail each other.

But that they keep returning, keep learning, keep practicing, and keep choosing the small and necessary things that help love endure.

If this little book leaves you with one lasting thought, let it be this:

A happy marriage is not found. It is built.

And it is built, day by day, with love — brick by brick.

Bonus: A One-Page Marriage Reset

When life gets busy, and your relationship starts to feel rushed, distant, or worn thin, return to these five simple questions:

1. Are we telling each other the truth?
2. Are we treating each other with courtesy?
3. Are we making time for companionship?
4. Are we showing daily care in visible ways?
5. Are we being consistent in the small things?

One honest conversation around these five questions can begin to restore closeness.

www.ingramcontent.com/pod-product-compliance
Lightning Source LLC
Chambersburg PA
CBHW022047150726
48196CB00075B/874/J

* 9 7 9 8 9 9 5 5 8 3 9 0 5 *